The Senses

By Paul Bennett

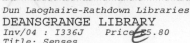 Belitha Press

For Henry

First published in Great Britain in 1997 by

Belitha Press Limited
London House, Great Eastern Wharf
Parkgate Road, London SW11 4NQ

This edition published in 1998. Reprinted in 1999

Copyright © Belitha Press Limited 1997
Text copyright © Paul Bennett

Editor: Veronica Ross
Series designer: Hayley Cove
Photographer: Claire Paxton
Illustrator: Cilla Eurich
Assistant designer: Sam King
Picture researcher: Diana Morris
Consultants: Elizabeth Atkinson/Jo Ormisher

ISBN 1 85561 780 3 (paperback)
ISBN 1 85561 836 2 (big book)
ISBN 1 85561 596 7 (hardback)

Printed in Hong Kong/China

Photo credits
Bubbles: 7t Geoff du Feu, 13t Jennie Woodcock, 18b Frans Rombout, 22t Rohith Jayawardine, 25t Frans Rombout. Mother & Baby Picture Library: 21t. Spectrum Colour Library: 19t. Zefa/Stockmarket: 8b, 12, 23, 27t.

Thanks to models Topel, Jodie, Bianca, Meera, Aimee, Spencer

Words in **bold** are explained in the list of useful words on pages 30 and 31.

Contents

Your brain and senses

Your brain is inside your head. It **controls** everything you do, from turning the pages of this book, to playing games, laughing, talking, thinking and moving.

Your brain takes in information and sends out messages to all parts of your body.

Your body sends messages back to your brain.

Some of the messages are about the things that you see, hear, smell, touch and taste. These are your five senses.

brain   skull

Your brain is very delicate. It is protected by your hard, bony **skull**.

5

The nervous system

Your **nervous system** is the link between your brain and your body.

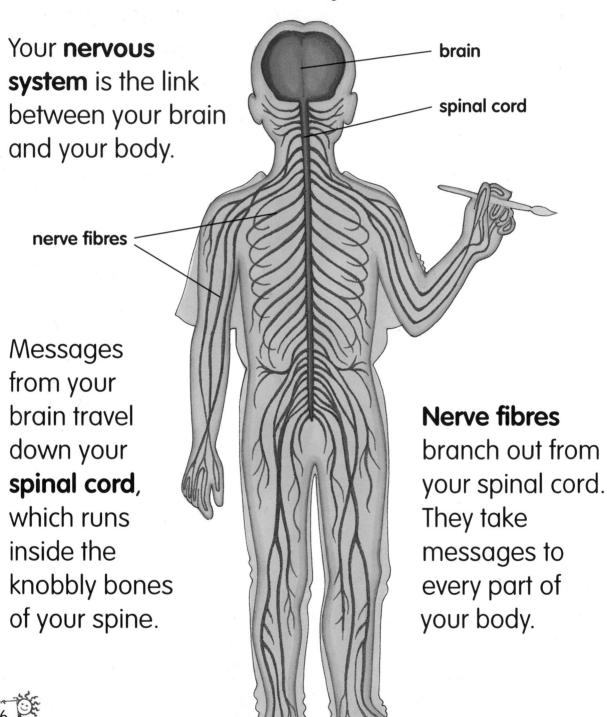

brain

spinal cord

nerve fibres

Messages from your brain travel down your **spinal cord**, which runs inside the knobbly bones of your spine.

Nerve fibres branch out from your spinal cord. They take messages to every part of your body.

6

When you read a computer screen, messages from your eyes are sent to your brain. Your brain works out what the words mean.

When you paint a picture, your brain sends messages to your arms and hands to tell them what to do.

7

How do I see?

You see with your eyes. They allow you to see the world in all its different colours.

Your eye is shaped like a ball, but you can only see the front part of it. The coloured part of your eye is the **iris**. The dark part is the **pupil**.

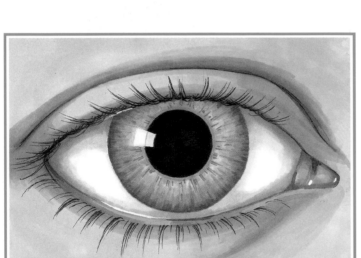

Light shines through your pupil and on to the back of your eye. Nerve **cells** in your eye send messages to your brain.

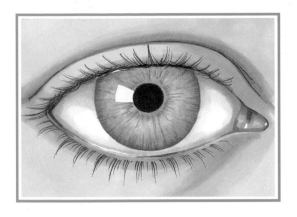

In bright light, your pupil is small to let in less light.

In dim light, your pupil is large to let in more light.

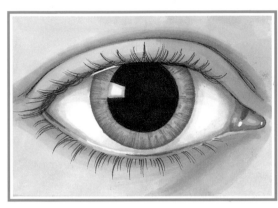

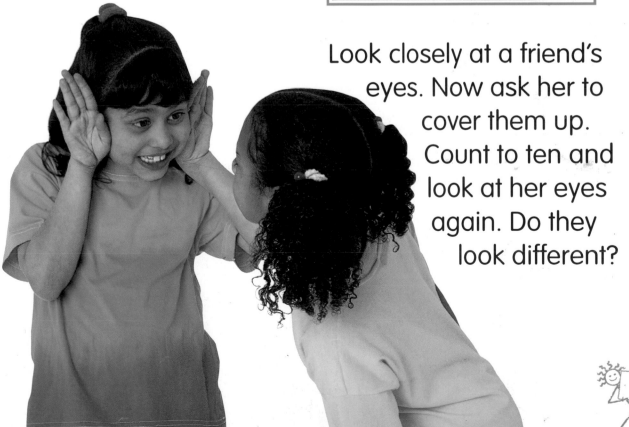

Look closely at a friend's eyes. Now ask her to cover them up. Count to ten and look at her eyes again. Do they look different?

How do I hear?

You hear with your ears. Your outer ear collects sounds, and sends them down a tube, called the ear canal, and into your head.

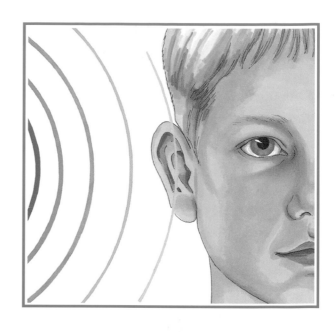

Inside your head, sound is turned into messages, which are sent to your brain.

Your brain tells you about the sounds you hear.

It tells you about the soft sound of a whisper, the loud sound of a car horn, the high ring of small bells, or the deep boom of a drum.

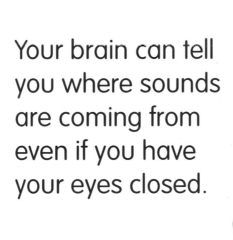

Your brain can tell you where sounds are coming from even if you have your eyes closed.

Taking care of your eyes and ears

You should take care of your eyes and ears because your sight and hearing are very **precious**.

When you are reading make sure that you have enough light.

Never look directly at the sun. Wear sunglasses to protect your eyes in bright sunshine.

If you cannot see clearly, you may need to wear glasses. The person who checks your eyes is called an optician.

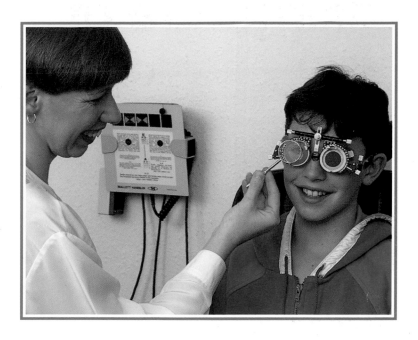

Very loud sounds can damage your hearing. People who work with loud machinery wear **ear protectors** for safety.

Never shout in someone's ear.

Bitter and sweet

Imagine what it would be like if you could not taste your favourite food or drink. Boring!

Your tongue is covered in thousands of tiny bumps, called taste buds.

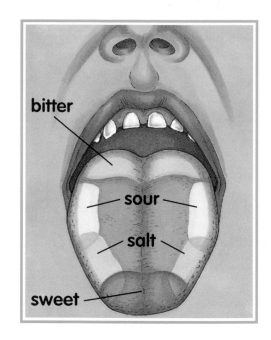

bitter

sour

salt

sweet

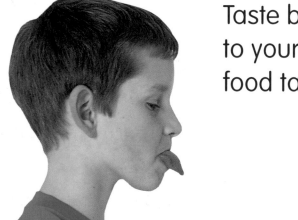

Taste buds send messages to your brain about what food tastes like.

Your tongue can sense
four tastes: sweet, sour,
salt and bitter.

Lemon juice is sour. You
can taste it at the side of
your tongue. Crisps and
peanuts are salty. These
are tasted at the side of
your tongue, too.

The taste buds at the back
of your tongue taste bitter
things like orange peel.

Chocolate is sweet and
is tasted by taste buds
at the tip of your tongue.

15

Smell

When you sniff hard, air goes up into your nose and messages about the smell are sent to your brain.

The scent of flowers, newly-mown grass and freshly-cooked bread are smells most people like.

Rotten eggs and unwashed socks smell horrible.

When you have a cold and your nose is blocked, you cannot taste your food properly.

This is because your sense of taste and smell work together.

Hold your nose while you eat. Can you taste the food properly?

Touching and feeling

The surface of your skin has millions of tiny **nerve endings**. These give you a sense of touch. Your skin tells you what things feel like.

Chips are hot.
Ice-cream is cold.
Tree trunks are rough.
Glue is sticky.
Slugs are slimy.
Wood is hard.

Rabbits have soft, smooth fur, which makes them nice to stroke.

Blind people learn to read using their sense of touch. The letters are made of patterns of tiny raised bumps. Blind people feel the bumps with the tips of their fingers. This pattern of bumps is called Braille.

Apples feel hard and smooth.

That hurts!

Pain is your body's way of telling you that something is wrong and that you should stop what you are doing.

Your fingertips and lips are very **sensitive** to pain, and to heat and cold. They will tell you when a drink is too hot, and needs to cool down.

Elbows are sensitive too. This mother is using her elbow to check that the water is not too hot before she bathes her baby.

When you fall over and bang your knees, nerve cells in your skin send pain messages to your brain and your knees hurt!

Your reflexes

What do you do when you touch something prickly, like a cactus? You jerk your hand away quickly. This is called a reflex action. Reflexes are actions you do without thinking.

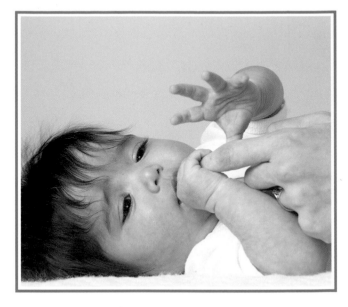

Babies have many reflex actions. If they are startled, they will throw out their arms to grab something.

Blinking and breathing are reflex actions, too. You can control these actions, but only for a short time.

Try this out. Hold your breath and count to 15, but try not to blink. Can you do it?

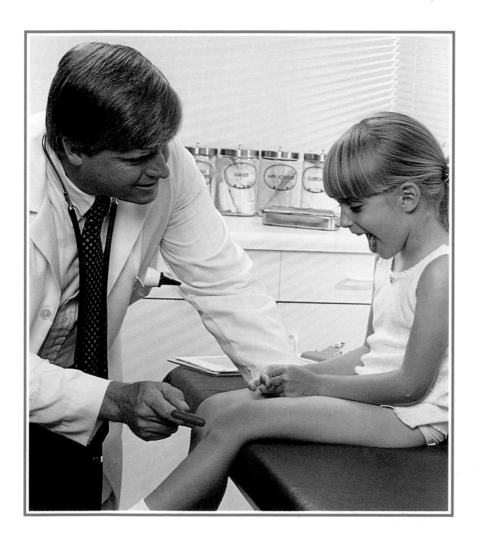

If a doctor taps your leg just below the knee, the bottom half of your leg jerks up. This is a reflex action.

23

Learning and memory

You begin to learn about the world as soon as you are born.

You learn to walk, talk, read and write when you are a child.

You learn many things by doing them again and again. When you learn to write, you need to **practise** making the shapes of the letters until you get them right.

When you learn to ride a bicycle, you must practise until you can do it without thinking.

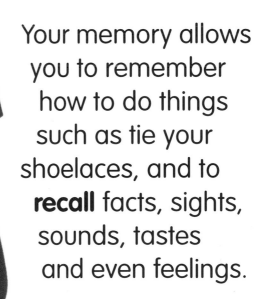

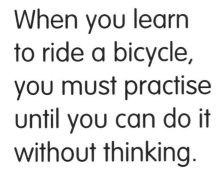

Your memory allows you to remember how to do things such as tie your shoelaces, and to **recall** facts, sights, sounds, tastes and even feelings.

A sense of balance

Can you stand
on one leg?
Your sense
of balance stops
you falling
over.

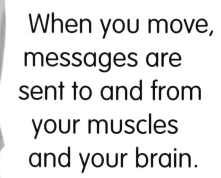

When you move,
messages are
sent to and from
your muscles
and your brain.

Messages from
your **inner ears**,
eyes, **muscles**
and other parts
of your body help
you to balance.

The messages
make sure that
the different parts
of your body move
together smoothly. This
is called co-ordination.

Acrobats need a good
sense of balance and
good co-ordination
to be able to form a
human pyramid, like
the one shown here.

Co-ordination allows
you to throw and catch
a ball, or juggle without
dropping anything.

27

Why do I need to sleep?

Sleep gives your body a chance to recover from all the tiring things you did during the day.

Babies sleep for about 16 hours a day. A 6-year-old sleeps for 10–11 hours a night. An adult sleeps for about 7–8 hours.

Do you remember your dreams?

We all dream, but no one really knows why. Some dreams are frightening.

If you have a bad dream, think about something nice, like a party or a holiday. Soon you will drift off to sleep again.

Some **scientists** think that dreams are the brain's way of sorting out all the new information it has taken in during the day.

29

Useful words

Cells
Tiny parts that make
up your body.

Controls
Directs things that happen.

Ear protectors
Special pads that are
worn over the ears to stop
them being damaged by
loud sounds.

Inner ears
The parts of your ear inside
your head that help you
to balance.

Iris
The coloured part of the
eye around the pupil.

Muscles
The soft, stretchy parts
inside your body that
make you move.

Nerve endings
Tiny parts in your skin that
tell you about the things
that you touch.

Nerve fibres
Long, thin threads that
carry messages from
all parts of your body
to your brain.

Nervous system
Nerves that branch out
from the spinal cord to
all parts of your body.

Practise
To do something again and again until you are good at it.

Precious
Very special.

Pupil
The middle of the eye, the part that you see through.

Recall
To remember or bring a memory into your mind.

Scientists
People who carry out investigations to find out how things happen.

Sensitive
To be able to tell the difference between things that are hot and cold, rough and smooth, sharp and soft, and so on.

Skull
The bony part of your head.

Spinal cord
A collection of nerves that run inside your backbone. The spinal cord takes messages from your brain to all parts of your body.

Index